AF624497

Where The Wildflowers Grow

Miranda Villareal

BookLeaf Publishing
India | USA | UK

Made with ❤ on the BookLeaf Publishing Platform
www.bookleafpub.in
www.bookleafpub.com

Dedication

To the souls who have loved me unconditionally,
through every season of growth—
Thank you.

Preface

If you're reading this,
I believe you are someone who has carried
the weight of pain and fear
long enough to stay open.
The bigger the space for sorrow,
the greater the room for joy.

Acknowledgements

1. Poem #1

Pain's presence
awakens us
from a long, cold winter.

2. Poem #2

Allowing pain in often feels
like a death.
As it travels through the body,
pain **unravels everything**–
the barriers that kept us hidden,
our darkness exposed.
The life we once knew
is seen for the last time.
And anything we once held onto
is gone,
making space
for light to enter–
the seeming nothingness.

3. Poem #3

The wisdom of trauma
instructs in a way nothing else can.
It strips, shatters, and disembodies,
planting us in the seeming nothingness—
like seeds buried deep in dark soil.
There, trauma transforms
into the light of wisdom,
growing from what once felt barren.
At first, it can feel scary;
the unfamiliar echo is so quiet,
compared to the anxiety,
the pain, the darkness,
the fear that once shadowed our growth.

4. Poem #4

Before you go,
take all your pieces with you;
for without you here,
they will feel heavy.
Before you leave,
remember that I was with you.
And if **it feels like** I am far now,
it is because I have called myself back.
My strength is now my own.
I can breathe, feel, laugh, and cry.
If there comes a time you miss me,
know that I was with you.

5. Poem #5

Even amidst deep healing,
my body still reminded me—
of a heartbreak anniversary.
Yoga helped twist
the memories from my body.
It **echoed** through muscle,
through breath,
urging me to keep going,
keep healing.

6. Poem #6

I cried and lay frozen in time,
and I accepted the words, "It's time to hold your feet to the fire."
The active acceptance of heartache
burns, and it's a wonder
at what point it may become unbearable.
My prayer for the day was simple:
I asked for my next breath of oxygen.
Breathing through heartache
feels like breathing through a marathon.
As I took in my breath,
I held my palms to the ground,
imagining the pain I could no longer hold
drain from my chest,
down my arms,
to my hands,
and into the depths of the earth.
And I imagined the earth
turning my pain into wildflowers.

7. Poem #7

Shedding the layers after **heartbreak**,
turn each season into something new and miraculous.
Hidden beauties are now found in the mundane;
the rose-colored goggles of heartache
now accentuate the colors of reality
in a beautiful way.
Each layer that goes
leaves you feeling lighter.
And as you become lighter,
you can now begin to hold space for others.

8. Poem #8

That day I told you I was busy,
it was because I had a haircut scheduled.
I needed a fresh start,
and I couldn't delay it any longer.
So I got a damn haircut
and dragged myself—and my fabulous hair—to therapy.

9. Poem #9

After the deepest soul sobbing,
the residual fear left me feeling
like a part of me was dying.
Every façade was stripped away by truth.
I lay on the floor, raw and naked,
with no way of being comforted.
And in that moment,
I realized my soul was homesick.

10. Poem #10

There was a season when I couldn't cry,
the communication within myself was disconnected.
Eloquence was far from me,
and connection felt foreign.
I had enough energy to get through the day,
then I'd fade into the couch,
trying to find the strength
to do it all over again tomorrow.
In emotional situations,
out of fight, flight, or freeze,
I'm the latter.
Frozen numbness is lonely and exhausting,
but sometimes it's needed for survival.
What gets you to the point of needing something drastic
to break free?

11. Poem #11

You brought it up first.
I thought it was a great opportunity,
excited for us to have a breakthrough.
Those unspoken expectations–
you taught me about them.
I didn't know that day
would drastically change my life.
The things I prayed for showed up,
without even knowing I was praying for them.
The cry from my soul hurt you,
but that cry freed me.

12. Poem #12

I thought I had reached some upper level of happiness,
and apparently, **I'd kept myself there** for quite some time.
It all comes down to what you believe you're worthy of.
I used to think that was all bullshit–
until I started really seeing myself
and loving who I was.
I remember the day so clearly–
I walked in high-vibe energy–
a magnet for love.
And that pull
has taken me places
beyond my wildest dreams.

13. Poem #13

Soul cries come from the ego dying,
while the quietness of rebirth
provides just enough stillness
to listen for all the mystery
you didn't know was possible.

14. Poem #14

If eyes could speak,
when I'm looking at you,
mine would say simply, "Thank you."
They'd end with the truth:
there aren't words in any language
to describe what they see,
as they try to hide a smile.
My eyes would tell you **the whole story**–
in a way my words never could.

15. Poem #15

Healing may be one of the most difficult journeys of life,
but if you choose it,
you become one of the bravest people in the world.
When you press in,
you strengthen the art of acceptance.
And that acceptance opens hidden doors,
and life begins to unfold,
as it was always meant to.

16. Poem #16

Let your garden speak for you,
let it whisper of the seeds you've sown in silence—
how, sometimes, you watered with quiet tears,
waiting patiently with the earth.
Your garden will tell the story—
you won't have to say a word.
When growth begins to show,
take it in without hurry.
There's no need to shout to the world,
you can sit alone in the peace of it,
or share its beauty with a friend.
The waiting has been enough,
the stillness has prepared you
for this moment—
to simply be.

17. Poem #17

If I were to tell myself a year ago
about **all the beautiful things** that would happen,
I don't know if she would believe me.
I wish I could hug her.
She was standing on ground zero,
after a world of illusions had just been deconstructed.
Illusions that needed to be revealed for what they were–
but that doesn't mean they come in a painless package.
I cried more during that time than I ever had before.
A lifetime of pain,
lifetimes of pain, finally being felt.
It's hard to look beyond pain,
but if I could go back to my past self,
I would tell her:
You are going to find hope in the unknown.
You are going to discover incredible things about
yourself
that you never knew.
You are going to let go of religion and accept the truth.
There will be healing to do in it all,
but this time you have yourself–your true self.
And you will realize that's all you've ever needed.

18. Poem #18

One of the first days I finally embraced the unknown,
I felt like I could finally take a deep breath.
My breathing had become shallow,
as I was unwilling to accept what was—
or what I thought everything should be.
But when **I learned to accept**,
I could finally breathe.
I went to the aquarium
and was mesmerized by the jellyfish—
these spineless beings,
embodying beauty by merging with matter,
making art with every move.
The water around them shimmered like liquid light,
and my chest opened with each pulse of their movement.
I could finally breathe, and I think the jellyfish danced a little more that day,
as if, in their stillness,
they had always known how to surrender.
So I let go too.
We shared in the quiet surrender of simply being.

19. Poem #19

Sometimes you don't realize how much you've changed
until you stand before a mirror,
choosing clothes that once felt foreign,
but now fit like skin–
as though you've been wearing them all along.
Your outer world begins to align
with the work you've done inside,
the way the body follows the mind's whisper,
the way the skin learns what it's meant to wear.
You'll wear new outfits that make you feel beautiful,
not because of the clothes themselves,
but **because they reveal what you've always been**–
the visual of what was hidden,
waiting beneath your skin.

20. Poem #20

Isn’t it beautiful
how, once you finally let go,
you find everything you've ever needed–
the words to describe your most perfect moments,
tears to express your deepest empathy,
love that overtakes your human body,
joy that burns, unending.
Isn’t it beautiful
how, **once you let go**,
life can show up for you in the most miraculous ways.

21. Poem #21

When your life begins to look different,
don't let it scare you.
Even when the places feel foreign,
and the faces unfamiliar,
dive in.
This is what it was all leading to—
every piece, every choice,
every person
helped you create this beautiful moment.
It's time to ask:
Show me how good this life can get.

www.ingramcontent.com/pod-product-compliance
Lightning Source LLC
Chambersburg PA
CBHW051719130826
49812CB00034B/1249
9789367395042